CHINESE SLANGUAGE

A *FUN* VISUAL GUIDE TO MANDARIN TERMS AND PHRASES BY MIKE ELLIS

GIBBS SMITH

First Edition
17 16 15   10 11

Text © 2010 Mike Ellis
Illustrations © 2010 Rupert Bottenberg

Published by
Gibbs Smith
P.O. Box 667
Layton, Utah 84041

1.800.835.4993 orders
www.gibbs-smith.com

Designed by Michel Vrana
Printed and bound in Hong Kong

Printed and bound in Hong Kong
Gibbs Smith books are printed on paper produced from sustainable PEFC-certified forest/controlled wood source. Learn more at www.pefc.org.

Library of Congress Cataloging-in-Publication Data

Ellis, Mike, 1961-
  Chinese slanguage : a fun visual guide to Mandarin terms and phrases / Mike Ellis. — 1st ed.
     p. cm.
  ISBN-13: 978-1-4236-0750-2
  ISBN-10: 1-4236-0750-3
  1. Chinese language—Conversation and phrase books—English. 2. Mandarin dialects. I. Title.
  PL1125.E6E45 2010
  495.1'83421—dc22
                                        2009032974

CONTENTS

I'd like to acknowledge all the folks at Gibbs Smith who were open-minded enough to take on a project like this.

And to my mom who instilled in me an appreciation for listening. My ability to listen has enabled me to teach anybody a new language using the language skills they already possess.

HOW TO USE THIS BOOK

If you want to learn the basics of Mandarin, but traditional methods seem overwhelming or intimidating, this book is for you! Just follow the directions below and soon you'll be able to say dozens of words and phrases in Mandarin.

• Follow the illustrated prompts and say the phrase quickly and smoothly with equal emphasis on the words or syllables. While Mandarin is a tonal language, you'll still be understood if you speak clearly and evenly.

• Learn to string together words or phrases to create many more phrases.

• Draw your own pictures to help with memorization and pronunciation.

Note: This product may produce Americanized Mandarin.

For free sound bytes, visit slanguage.com

GREETINGS AND RESPONSES

Hello
喂　*wèi*

Way

Hi
嗨　*hēi*

Hey

Thanks
谢谢　*xiè xie*

Shay Shay

Thanks, you too
谢谢，你也一样
xiè xie, nǐ yě yí yàng

Shay Shay Knee Yay E Yawng

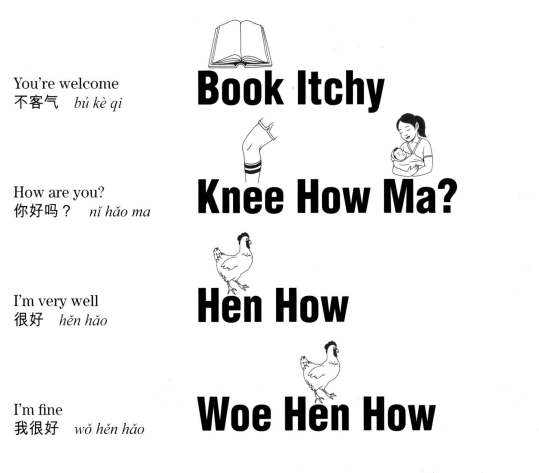

You're welcome
不客气　*bú kè qi*

Book Itchy

How are you?
你好吗？　*nǐ hǎo ma*

Knee How Ma?

I'm very well
很好　*hěn hǎo*

Hen How

I'm fine
我很好　*wǒ hěn hǎo*

Woe Hen How

Not very well
不太好   *bù tài hǎo*

Boo Tie How

I don't know
我不知道
wǒ bù zhī dào

Woe Boots Dow

Okay
好，没问题
hǎo, méi wèn tí

How May Win Tee

Okay?
没问题吗
méi wèn tí ma

May Win Tee Ma?

Beer
啤酒 *pí jiǔ*

Pea Joe

Coffee
咖啡 *kā fēi*

Café

Milk
牛奶 *niú nǎi*

Nyo Nye

Wine
酒 *jiǔ*

Joe

Fish
鱼 *yú*

You

Pancake
薄烤饼 *báo kǎo bǐng*

B'Ow Cow Bing

Soup
汤 *tāng*

Tong

Beef
牛肉 *niú ròu*

Nyo Row

Meat
肉 *ròu*

Row

Spinach
菠菜 *bō cài*

Boat Sigh

French fries
炸薯条 *zhá shǔ tiáo*

Jaw Shoe Tee-Ow

Vegetable
蔬菜 *shū cài*

Shoot Sigh

Peas
豌豆 *wān dòu*

One Doe

Rice
米 *mǐ*

Me

Egg
蛋 *dàn*

Don

Radish
萝卜 *luó bo*

L'Whoa Bow

Blackberry
黑莓　*hēi méi*

Hay May

Pear
梨　*lí*

Lee

Turkey
火鸡　*huǒ jī*

Hoe Jee

Candy
糖果　*táng guǒ*

Tong Go

Dinner
晚餐 *wǎn cān*

Want Son

Pants Uh

Plate
盘子 *pán zi*

Bowl
碗 *wǎn*

Wan

Delicious
美味的 *měi wèi de*

May Wade

Arm
手臂　*shǒu bì*

Tooth
牙齿　*yá chǐ*

Back
背脊　*bèi jǐ*

Stomach
胃　*wèi*

Show Bee

Yachts

Bay Gee

Way

Knee
膝盖 *xī gài*

She Guy

Throat
喉咙 *hóu lóng*

Hoe Long

Hand
手 *shǒu*

Show

Nose
鼻子 *bí zi*

Beads

Foot
脚 *jiǎo*

Gee-Ow

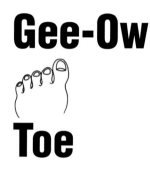

Head
头 *tóu*

Toe

Face
脸 *liǎn*

Leeann

Skin
皮肤　*pí fū*

Pea Foo

Ton Boo

Hip
臀部　*tún bù*

Brow
眉毛　*méi mao*

Maim Ow

To sneeze
打喷嚏 *dǎ pēn tì*

Da Pun Tee

She

To wash
洗 *xǐ*

Moo You

A bath
沐浴 *mù yù*

A shower
淋浴 *lín yù*

Lean You

To choke
阻塞 *zǔ sè*

Pulse
脉搏 *mài bó*

Breathing
呼吸 *hū xī*

Zoo Suh

My Bow

Who She

To have
拥有　*yōng yǒu*

Yong Yo

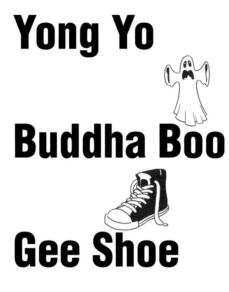

To have to
不得不　*bù dé bù*

Buddha Boo

To describe
记述　*jì shù*

Gee Shoe

To ask
问　*wèn*

When

To sleep
睡觉 *shuì jiào*

Shoe-Eh Gee-Ow

To send
送 *sòng*

Song

To smell
闻 *wén*

Win

To surround
围绕 *wéi rào*

Way Rrr-Ow

To see
看 *kàn*

Khan

To offer
提供 *tí gōng*

Tee Gong

To read
读 *dú*

Due

To leave
离开 *lí kāi*

Leek I

To understand
理解 *lǐ jiě*

Lee Gee-Eh

To depend
依靠 *yī kào*

Eek Ow

To give back
归还 *guī huán*

Gway Juan

To bend
弯曲 *wān qū*

Want Chu

To annoy
烦恼　*fán nǎo*

Fawn Now

To disobey
违背　*wéi bèi*

Way Bay

To wash
洗　*xǐ*

She

To boil
沸腾　*fèi téng*

Fay Tongue

Enough
足够 *zú gòu*

Zoo Go

Also
也 *yě*

Yay

Of course
当然 *dāng rán*

Dong Ron

Well
好 *hǎo*

How

Badly
坏 *huài*

Too much
太多 *tài duō*

At all
根本 *gēn běn*

Usually
通常 *tōng cháng*

Why

Tie Do-Whoa

Gun Bun

Tong Cha-Ung

After
后来　*hòu lái*

Hoe Lie

Better
更好　*gèng hǎo*

Gung How

Silently
默默地　*mò mò de*

Moe Moe Duh

Inside
内部 *nèi bù*

Nay Boo

Somewhere
某处 *mǒu chù*

Moe Chew

Bad
坏 *huài*

Why

Good
好 *hǎo*

How

Sad
悲哀 *bēi āi*

Bay Eye

Clumsy
笨拙 *bèn zhuō*

Bung Whoa

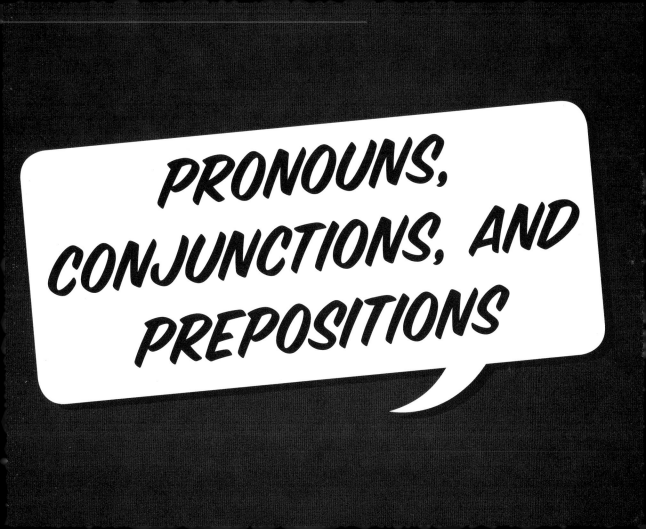

You
你 *nǐ*

Knee

Who
谁 *sheí*

Shay

All
所有 *suǒ yǒu*

Ss-whoa Yo

But
但是 *dàn shì*

Don Shh!

Near
邻近 *lín jìn*

Lean Jean

Behind
后面 *hòu mian*

Homey An

Nay Boo

Inside
内部 *nèi bù*

Also
也 *yě*

Yay

Just
刚刚 *gāng gāng*

Gong Gong

And
和 *hé*

Huh?

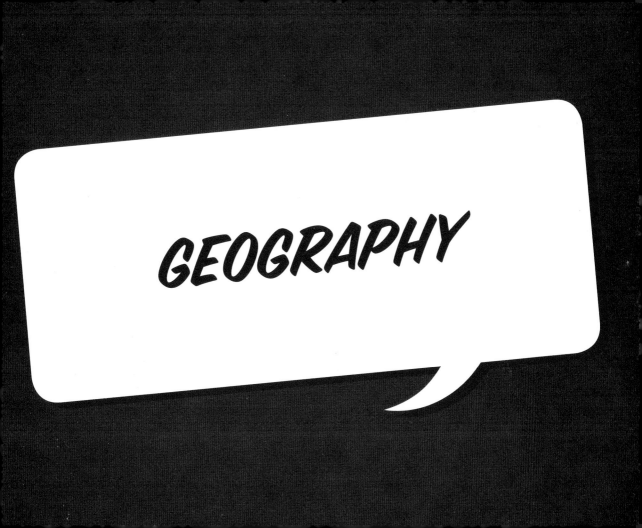

United States
美国 *měi guó*

Western
西方 *xī fāng*

West
西 *xī*

Meg Whoa

She Fang

She

East
东 *dōng*

Dong

North
北 *běi*

Bay

South
南 *nán*

Non

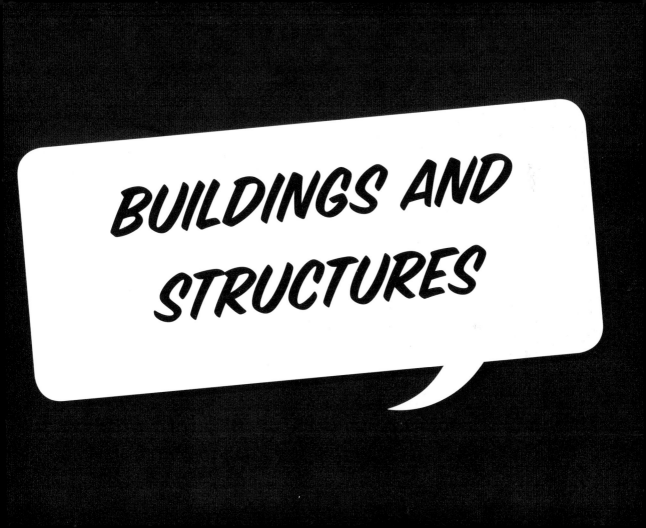

Restaurant
餐馆 *cān guǎn*

Song One

Temple
庙 *miào*

Meow

Prison
监狱 *jiān yù*

Gee-Uhn You

Bridge
桥 *qiáo*

Chi-Ow

It's hot
天气很热
tiān qì hěn rè

Tee Ann She Henry

It's sunny out
外面阳光明媚
wài miàn yáng
guāng míng mèi

Why Me-Ann Yon Wong Ming May

It's raining
下雨了
xià yǔ le

She-Ah You Luh

ENTERTAINMENT AND THE ARTS

Cartoon
卡通　*kǎ tōng*

Cat Tongue

Theater
电影院　*diàn yǐng yuàn*

Diane 'n You Win

Play
剧本　*jù běn*

Jew Bun

Guitar
吉他　*jí tā*

Gee Ta

Violin
小提琴　*xiǎo tí qín*

She-Ow Teaching

Flute
笛子　*dí zi*

Deez Uh

Painting
绘画　*huì huà*

Who-Eh Who-Ah

Comedy
喜剧　*xǐ jù*

She Jew

Daughter
女儿　*nǚ ér*

New Are

Grandmother
祖母　*zǔ mǔ*

Zoo Moo

Grandfather
祖父　*zǔ fù*

Zoo Foo

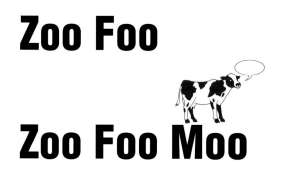

Grandparents
祖父母　*zǔ fù mǔ*

Zoo Foo Moo

Granddaughter
孙女　*sūn nǚ*

Soon Knew

Grandchildren
孙子　*sūn zi*

Soon's Uh

A couple
夫妻　*fū qī*

Foo Chi

A descendant
后代　*hòu dài*

Hoe Die

Son
儿子 *ér zi*

Er's Uh

Grandson
孙子 *sūn zi*

Soon's Uh

Mother
母亲 *mǔ qīn*

Moo Cheen

Father
父亲 *fù qīn*

Foo Cheen

Brother
兄弟 *xiōng dì*

She-Ong Dee

Sister
姐妹 *jiě mèi*

Gee-Eh May

Aunt
姨妈 *yí mā*

Ye Ma

Uncle
伯父 *bó fù*

Bow Foo

Sad
悲哀 *bēi āi*

Bay Eye

Pain
疼痛 *téng tòng*

Tung Tong

Interested
有兴趣 *yǒu xìng qù*

Yo Sheeng Chew

Happy
幸福的 *xìng fú de*

Sheeng Foo Duh

Angry
愤怒的 *fèn nù de*

Fun Nude

Bored
无聊的 *wú liáo de*

Woo Lee Out

Tired
疲乏的　*pí fá de*

Pea Fa Duh

Hungry
饥饿的　*jī è de*

Gee Uh Duh

Nice
亲切的　*qīn qiè de*

Cheen Chi-Eh Duh

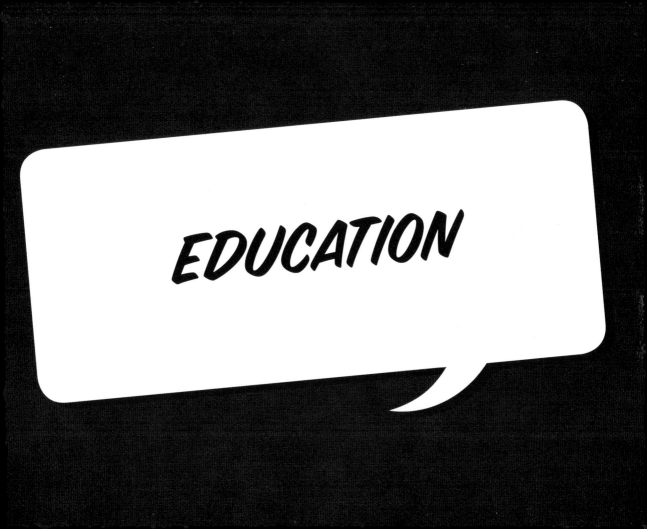

To count
计算 *jì suàn*

Gee Sue-Ann

A question mark
问号 *wèn hào*

When How

Chalk
粉笔 *fěn bǐ*

Fun Bee

Summer
夏天 *xià tiān*

She-Ought Ian

School
学校　*xué xiào*

Shoe-Eh She-Ow

Classroom
教室　*jiào shì*

Gee-Ow Shuh

Teacher
老师　*lǎo shī*

L'Ow Shuh

Student
学生　*xué shēng*

Shoe-Eh Shung

Book
书本 *shū běn*

Shoe Ben

Exam
考试 *kǎo shì*

Cow Shuh

Homework
作业 *zuò yè*

Z'Whoa Yay

Notebook
笔记本 *bǐ jì běn*

Bee Gee Ben

Semester
学期 *xué qī*

Shway Chi

Holiday
假期 *jià qī*

Gee-Ah Chi

College or university
大学 *dà xué*

Dah Shway

An evening
傍晚 *bàng wǎn*

Bong One

A minute
分 *fēn*

Fun

A second
秒 *miǎo*

Meow

The future
未来 *wèi lái*

Way Lie

Mountain
山 *shān*

Shawn

Fire
火 *huǒ*

Whoa

Sun
太阳 *tài yáng*

Tie Young

Rain
雨 *yǔ*

You

Ocean
海洋 *hǎi yáng*

Sea
大海 *dà hǎi*

Beach
海滩 *hǎi tān*

Lake
湖 *hú*

Hi Young

Dah Hi

Hi Tahn

Who

Tree
树木 *shù mù*

A pine
松树 *sōng shù*

Fish
鱼 *yú*

Dog
狗 *gǒu*

Shoe Moo

Song Shoe

You

Go

Mouse
鼠 *shǔ*

Shoe

Tiger
虎 *hǔ*

Who

Camel
骆驼 *luò tuo*

L'Whoa T'Whoa

Dolphin
海豚 *hǎi tún*

Hi Twin

Horse
马　*mǎ*

Ma

Seagull
海鸥　*hǎi ōu*

High Oh

Hen
母鸡　*mǔ jī*

Moo Gee

Belt
皮带 *pí dài*

Pea Die

Blouse
上衣 *shàng yī*

Sean Gee

Swimsuit
泳衣 *yǒng yī*

Young Ye

Scarf
围巾 *wéi jīn*

Way Jean

Sweater
毛衣 *máo yī*

Mao Ye

Handkerchief
手帕 *shǒu pà*

Show Pa

Shawl
披肩　*pī jiān*

Pea Gee-Ann

Umbrella
伞　*sǎn*

Sahn

Jumper
背心　*bèi xīn*

Bay Sheen

To go
去　*qù*

Chew

To cross
横过　*héng guò*

Hung Whoa

To come back
回来　*huí lái*

Who-Eh Lie

To drive
驱赶　*qū gǎn*

Chew Gone

A purchase
购买　*gòu mǎi*

Go My

To buy/sell
买　*mǎi*

My

A receipt
收据　*shōu jù*

Show Jew

A list
目录　*mù lù*

Moo Loo

To play
玩　*wán*

One

A game
游戏　*yóu xì*

Yo She

Balance
均衡　*jūn héng*

June Hung

Run
跑步　*pǎo bù*

Pow Boo

Jog
漫步 *màn bù*

Man Boo

Baseball
棒球 *bàng qiú*

Bong Chi-Oh

Football
美式足球 *měi shì zú qiú*

Maish Zoo Chi-Oh

Soccer
英式足球 *yīng shì zú qiú*

Ingsh Zoo Chi-Oh

Skating
溜冰 *liū bīng*

Lee-Oh Being

Swimming
游泳 *yóu yǒng*

Yo Young

Hotel
旅馆 *lǚ guǎn*

Loo Gone

Airport
机场 *jī chǎng*

Gee Cha-Ung

Cab or Taxi
计程车 *jì chéng chē*

Gee Chung Cha

Bus
公共汽车
gōng gòng qì chē

Gong Gong Chi Cha

Ticket
车票 *chē piào*

Cha Pea-Ow

Restaurant
餐馆 *cān guǎn*

Son Gone

Bank
银行 *yín háng*

Ian Hang

MIKE ELLIS is a web designer who runs the popular website www.slanguage.com. He lives with his family in Philadelphia.